Index Card Games for ESL

Revised by

Raymond C. Clark

PRO LINGUA  ASSOCIATES

Pro Lingua Associates, Publishers
P.O.Box 1348
Brattleboro, Vermont 05302-1348 USA
Office: 802 257 7779
Orders: 800 366 4775
Fax: 802 257 5117
WWW. ProLingua Associates.com
Email: info@ProLingua Associates.com
        orders@ProLingua Associates.com
SAN: 216-0579

At **Pro Lingua**
our objective is to foster an approach
to learning and teaching that we call
interplay, *the* **inter***action of language*
learners and teachers with their materials,
with the language and culture,
and with each other in active, creative
and productive **play**.

Copyright © 2002, 2006 Pro Lingua Associates, Third Edition
Previous editions copyrighted by the Experiment in International Living

ISBN 0-86647-158-8: 978-0-86647-158-9

This book was set in a font called Bookman Old Style, a computer adaptation by Adobe of the Neoclassical type faces by such 18th Century masters as Pierre Simon Fournier and John Baskerville. The illustrations are by Patrick R. Moran. The book and cover designs are by Arthur A. Burrows. Printing and binding are by McNaughton and Gunn of Saline, Michigan.

Printed in the United States of America
Third Edition, Third printing 2012
There are 23,000 copies in print.

Contents

E = easy   *M* = moderate   *D* = difficult

Contents, *continued*

Introduction

The ordinary index card with a word, a phrase, or a sentence on it has been a proven success in the classroom for many years. This collection is the starting point for what could be an extensive collection of index card games for you or for your department, and in this edition, there are dozens of games ready to be photocopied, cut out, and pasted on cards for a variety of enjoyable and useful activities. There are clear and concise directions for how to use the various games. The games in this book, however, should also serve as examples of games that you, the teacher, can create to fit your own teaching situation. All you need, in addition to a copier, scissors, and paste is a supply of 3x5 index cards. Once created, the games can be used over and over again.

The games can be one of the most enjoyable supplementary activities that you can do with your class, whether you use them once a week or once a day. In an intensive language program you can easily use them once a day and the students will not tire of them. Because the games are a supplementary activity, they are best used to review or practice material that has already been introduced. In a limited way, however, they can be used to introduce new bits and pieces of language — especially vocabulary items and idioms.

Beyond the fact that the games are fun and a welcome change of pace, they are also useful. They can serve as a painless review of previously studied material. They are also invaluable in helping build the class into a cohesive group, as long as the competitive aspect of the games is not taken too seriously. In several of the games, groups of students have to work together toward a common goal, whether it be solving a problem, or building up points and trying to win. In the process of working together, the students necessarily have to interact with each other to help, support, suggest, encourage, share, and even correct and challenge each other. Inevitably, some teasing, joking, cheering, and play pervade the classroom. In short, the games give everyone, teacher included, a chance to play and be playful. In the language classroom, play is useful.

These games are useful in one other important way — they remove you, the teacher, from the spotlight and allow the students to deal with each other, the cards, and the language in front of them. You are there, of course. You get things started and add up the score and serve as the impartial referee, but you can stay out of the way for a while and let the players play. As they play, they are using the target langue in meaningful communication.

Throughout the book we have graded our games as easy, moderate, and difficult, but please accept these labels with the understanding that they are not rigid. The more important point is that the games can be enjoyed by students at all levels. After some experience you will develop a good sense for what your class can and can't do.

Have fun!

Acknowledgements

Our original collection of index card games was put together by members of the English language program faculty at the School for International Training. They are Marilyn Bean Barrett, Joe Bennett, Ruthanne Brown, Robert Carvutto, Jan Gaston, Harland Harris, Bonnie Mennell, Oden Oak, Phil Stantial, Elizabeth Tannenbaum, and Susan Treadgold.

World Learning, Inc., formerly the Experiment in International Living, has granted permission to Pro Lingua Associates to publish and revise the original, unpublished manuscript.

Person, Place, or Thing?

Brief Description:

This is a variation of "Twenty Questions." The number of questions is reduced to ten, and the field includes nouns that represent a person, a place, or a thing. The class is divided into two teams, and each team takes turns trying to guess the identity of one of the opposing players.

Purpose:

This game will require the students to practice yes-no questions. It can also serve as a vocabulary review and a challenge of general knowledge.

Preparation:

Use the sample sets of cards on the following pages, or write sets you create, each set having three cards and each card with the name of a person, a place, or a thing. On the person card, it may be necessary to provide some additional information.

Procedure:

1. Describe the cards to the students. Tell them there are three categories: person, place, or thing. Within each category in the sample sets, there are three levels: easy, moderate and difficult. To play the basic ten-question game, have the students choose which level they want to try.

2. Divide the class into two teams and give each player a card. Emphasize that the questions can only be yes-no questions, and the respondent answers only with "yes" or "no." Explain that only ten questions may be asked. The players may show their cards to others on their team.

3. A player from one team is quizzed by the other team. The questioning begins with "Are you a person?" etc., and continues until a correct identification has been made or ten questions have been answered.

4. The team with the most correct identifications wins.

Person, Place, or Thing

Variations:

1. Set a time limit on each ten-question session. A three-minute egg timer is useful for this.

2. Give each student a blank card, tell them a category (for example, a place or, more specifically, an island), and have them make up an item for their card. Check the results. If two or more students have written the same word, you should quietly ask them to change the duplicates.

3. Reverse the procedure by putting one student on the spot. Let every one else know what the word is, and have the student ask yes-no questions to the others.

4. You can also set the game up somewhat like *Jeopardy*, using the diagram below and nine cards like the samples in this book.

	PERSON	PLACE	THING
$5.00 EASY			
$10.00 MODERATE			
$20.00 DIFFICULT			

In this variation, you select and hold nine cards, three from each category. The students quiz you, operating as two teams. A student from one team says, for example, "I'll take a person for $10.00." You take a person card, and they ask you yes/no questions until they guess the person or get a "no." Then the other team takes over. They can continue trying to identify the same person or choose another square.

Draw the grid on the board and, as the game progresses, write the correct answers in the grid with the team's name, as below:

	PERSON	PLACE	THING
$5.00	Muhammad Ali TEAM A		
$10.00		Berlin TEAM B	
$20.00	Richard Nixon TEAM B		Blender TEAM A

The copyable games have been set up as sets of nine to allow for this variation.

Suggestions:

People

1. Professions
2. Social roles
   (parent, friend, relative, etc.)
3. Rock stars
4. Movie actors
5. American presidents
6. National leaders
7. Famous writers
8. Athletes
9. Local personalities*

Places

1. Countries
2. Cities
3. Rivers
4. Oceans, Seas
5. Islands
6. Mountains
7. Stores
8. Land forms
9. Local streets,
   buildings, parks, etc.*

Things

1. Classroom items
2. Household items
3. Kitchen tools
4. Appliances
5. Vehicles
6. Clothing
7. Office equipment
8. Sports equipment
9. Musical instruments*

Photocopyable sample games on most of these topics are included on the following pages. Those marked * are not included.

	Person	Place	Thing
Easy	Doctor	Russia	Desk
Moderate	Judge	Poland	Eraser
Difficult	Accountant	Albania	Index Card
Easy	Brother	London	Sofa
Moderate	Parent	Berlin	Curtain
Difficult	Nephew	Buenos Aires	Carpet
Easy	Mick Jagger	Amazon River	Frying Pan
Moderate	Paul McCartney	Missouri River	Can Opener
Difficult	ABBA	Nile River	Blender

4

Level	Person	Place	Thing
Easy	Marilyn Monroe	Pacific Ocean	TV
Moderate	Marlon Brando	Mediterranean Sea	Dishwasher
Difficult	Charlie Chaplin	Arctic Ocean	Coffee Maker
Easy	Nurse	China	Pen
Moderate	Lawyer	New Zealand	Wastebasket
Difficult	Surgeon	Zimbabwe	Pointer
Easy	Sister	Rome	Bed
Moderate	Aunt	Cairo	Dresser
Difficult	Friend	Istanbul	Bath Tub

	Person	Place	Thing
Easy	John Lennon	Mississippi River	Knife
Moderate	Madonna	The Thames	Measuring Cup
Difficult	KISS	Volga River	Spatula
Easy	Harrison Ford	Atlantic Ocean	Refrigerator
Moderate	Jane Fonda	Indian Ocean	DVD Player
Difficult	Ronald Reagan	Red Sea	Vacuum Cleaner
Easy	George Washington	Sicily	Bus
Moderate	Franklin Roosevelt	Madagascar	Motorcycle
Difficult	Harry Truman	Corsica	Jet Ski

	Person	Place	Thing
Easy	Winston Churchill	Mount Everest	Shirt
Moderate	Mikhail Gorbachev	Kilimanjaro	Jacket
Difficult	Ataturk	The Matterhorn	Vest
Easy	Shakespeare	Supermarket	Computer
Moderate	Mark Twain	Shoe Store	Filing Cabinet
Difficult	Cervantes	Pharmacy	Pencil Sharpener
Easy	Michael Jordan	Mountain	Basketball
Moderate	Muhammad Ali	Valley	Baseball Glove
Difficult	Pele	Plain	Ski Pole

Matched Pairs

Brief Description:

Similar to the TV show "Concentration," these games require the students to remember the location of the cards and make matching pairs. The game can be played as a team activity.

Purpose:

To review vocabulary. Sometimes new words can be added to the set, as long as the number of new words is small and not disruptive. A second purpose, if the game is played as a team activity, is to stimulate conversation among the team members: "I think seven matches twenty-three," or, "Do you remember where _____ is?" Finally, the game, like all the card games, is fun and contributes to group building.

Preparation:

From the samples or your imagination, choose a category, for example, antonyms. Write or paste a word on each of 12 cards and the matching antonym on another 12 cards. Shuffle the cards well, turn them over, and number them from 1 to 24 on the back.

Because the purpose of this game is to review something that has been taught, rather than teach something new, go over the pairs before the game begins to be sure everybody knows what the 12 pairs are. Alternatively, if you feel the students should know the words, just tell them what the general subject or topic is.

Procedure:

1. Lay the cards out face down with the numbers showing, as in figure 1.

2. Taking turns, the students call out two numbers, for example, 1 and 3.

3. Turn over the called pair of cards. If the cards don't match (chances are they won't for the first few turns), the cards are turned back over. In figure 2, "big" and "deep" don't match, so they should be turned face down again.

1	2	3	4	5	6
7	8	9	10	11	12
13	14	15	16	17	18
19	20	21	22	23	24

Figure 1

Figure 2

big	2	deep	4	5	6
7	8	9	10	11	12
13	14	15	16	17	18
19	20	21	22	23	24

big	2	3	4	5	6
7	8	9	10	11	12
13	14	15	little	17	18
19	20	21	22	23	24

Figure 3

4. When a student makes a match (figure 3), they remove the matched cards from the lay-out and they get another turn. They continue until they fail to produce a match.

5. When all the cards have been matched, the student with the most matches wins.

Matched Pairs

Variations:

1. The game can be played as a team activity. One person from each team is the spokesperson for the team's collective effort to remember locations. Students can take turns being the spokesperson.

2. When a match is made, the player can be required to use the words in a sentence. If the player fails to do so, the cards are returned to the lay-out, and the next player gets the opportunity to match and use the words.

Suggestions:

1. Synonyms*

2. Antonyms*

3. Phrasal verbs*

4. Homonyms

5. Same vowel sounds

6. Same beginning or ending sounds

7. Proverbs*

8. Idioms*

9. Compound words (ex. base — ball)

10. Countries and corresponding languages or capitals

11. Prefixes and bases * (ex. mis — understand)

12. Verb forms: simple and past; past and past participle

13. Pictures of objects and corresponding words*

* *Photocopyable sample games on these topics are included on the following pages.*

Adjective Synonyms

big	large
near	close
sick	ill
simple	easy
little	small
quick	fast
right	correct
difficult	hard
tall	high
happy	glad
angry	mad
many	a lot of

Adjective Synonyms

shy	timid
afraid	scared
huge	very large
slender	thin
well-known	famous
wealthy	rich
lucky	fortunate
intelligent	smart
amusing	funny
enough	sufficient
terrible	awful
total	complete

Adjective Synonyms

skeptical	doubtful
eccentric	strange
courageous	brave
nervous	anxious
calm	tranquil
candid	frank
truthful	honest
jealous	envious
careful	cautious
precise	exact
enormous	huge
sincere	earnest

Adjective Antonyms

old	new
little	big
fat	thin
cold	hot
wet	dry
high	low
warm	cool
good	bad
old	young
happy	sad
far	near
wide	narrow

Adjective Antonyms

polite	rude
huge	tiny
full	empty
light	heavy
long	short
clean	dirty
dead	alive
handsome	ugly
strong	weak
sharp	dull
single	married
smooth	rough

Adjective Antonyms

upset	calm
boring	fascinating
hasty	careful
peaceful	belligerent
rare	common
straight	crooked
plain	fancy
scarce	plentiful
gorgeous	ugly
generous	stingy
odd	even
liberal	conservative

Clothing

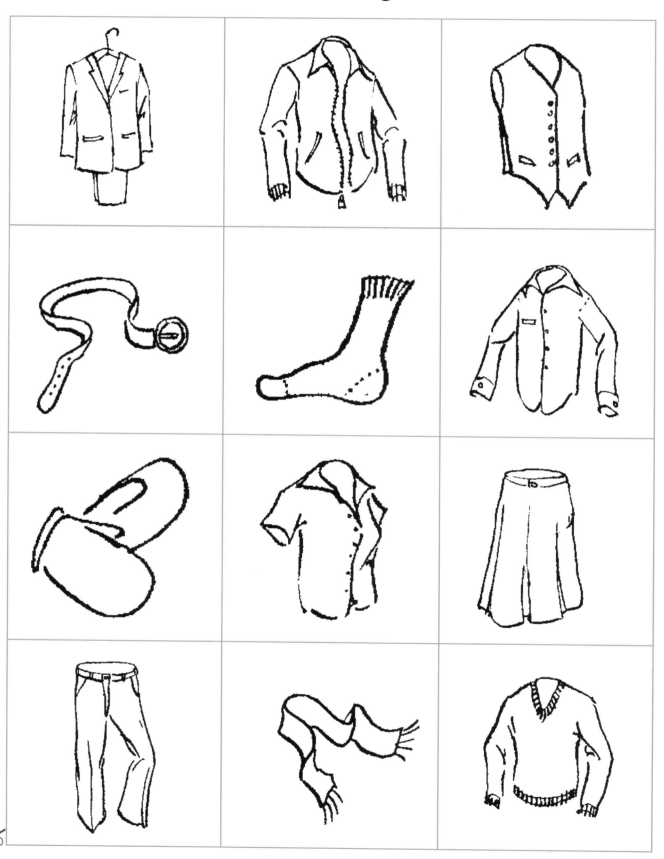

Clothing

suit
jacket
vest
belt
sock
shirt
mittens
blouse
skirt
pants
scarf
sweater

Phrasal Verbs: separable

pick out	choose
put on	dress
give back	return
take off	remove
talk over	discuss
do over	repeat
fill out	complete
find out	discover
look over	examine
leave out	omit
call off	cancel
put back	replace

Phrasal Verbs: inseparable

come back	return
call on	visit
look after	take care of
look like	resemble
get over	recover
wait on	serve
pick on	bother
run over	hit by a car
go over	review
look into	investigate
get along with	be friendly with
run out of	consume completely

Phrasal Verbs: all types

show up	appear
take up	begin to study
make up	create
bring up	raise children
put out	extinguish
pass out	faint
figure out	solve
put off	postpone
turn in	go to bed
throw away	discard
look up to	respect
talk back to	respond rudely

Adjective Synonyms: human qualities

courteous	polite
shy	bashful
beautiful	lovely
rude	impolite
humorous	funny
adolescent	juvenile
confident	sure
stupid	foolish
immature	childish
diligent	hard-working
conceited	stuck up
up-tight	anxious

Prefixes: negation, opposition

	mis	pronounce
	mis	understand
	dis	agree
	dis	ability
	un	pleasant
	un	fortunate
	in	dependent
	im	polite
	im	possible
	anti	terrorism
	mal	practice
	non	sense

Idioms

on purpose	intentionally
as a rule	usually
on hand	available
in fact	really
never mind	don't worry
by all means	certainly
no wonder	not surprising
right away	immediately
for good	permanently
by the way	incidentally
out of order	not working
off and on	occasionally

Proverbs

Don't cry	over spilled milk.
All that glitters	is not gold.
One who hesitates	is lost.
Where there's a will	there's a way.
Still waters	run deep.
Don't judge a book	by its cover.
Too many cooks	spoil the broth.
A stitch in time	saves nine.
One who laughs last	laughs best.
Time	heals all wounds.
Better late	than never.
Easier said	than done.

Sound and Spell

Brief Description:

Each card has one word written on it and one sound underlined, for example, br<u>ie</u>f. A set of 36 cards contains from two to six different sounds. The cards are shuffled and given to the students, who sort them into separate piles, one pile for each different sound.

Purpose:

The students review the pronunciation of selected words and sounds and the various ways the sounds can be spelled.

Preparation:

Select sounds that the students need to practice, for example, /iy/, as in "sheep," and /i/, as in "ship." Either use the sample sets on the following pages, or on a blank set of cards, write a number of words, each containing one of the sounds you have chosen to work on. If you are making the cards, underline the spelling of the sounds in question. Select a variety of troublesome spellings, for example:

<table>
<tr><td>gr<u>ee</u>n</td><td>fi<u>e</u>ld</td><td>n<u>ea</u>t</td></tr>
<tr><td>pol<u>i</u>ce</td><td>p<u>eo</u>ple</td><td>rec<u>ei</u>ve</td></tr>
</table>

A duplicate set should be prepared for each group of students. In general, students can do this game in groups of 3 to 5. To keep the sets from being mixed up, put each set in an envelope, or write a set number on the back.

Sound and Spell

Procedure:

1. Give the directions to the class. For example, "You have 36 cards in this set. There are three different sounds underlined. Read the words, pronounce them, and sort them into three piles."

2. Let the students work on the sounds and spellings. Do not give any help.

3. When all groups have finished their sorting, have the groups lay out their cards and look at each other's solutions.

4. Check the solutions and announce the winner(s) — the team with the most correct cards wins.

Variations:

1. To make the game more challenging, put one or two "wild cards" in each set — sounds that are completely different from the others.

2. Establish a time limit to the game. A three-minute egg timer is useful for this and other timed activities.

3. Instead of sounds and spellings, work on word stress. The students sort the words into piles with the primary stress on the 1st syllable, 2nd syllable and 3rd syllable. There is one example of this type of game in the following collection. (See page 37.)

Suggestions:

1. vowels and diphthongs*

2. consonants

3. regular past tense endings*

4. regular plural endings*

5. minimal pairs, for example, "ship/sheep, lip/leap, bit/beat," etc.

6. syllable stress*

*** Photocopyable sample games on these topics are included on the following pages.**

/i/	/iy/	/ay/
s<u>i</u>t	gr<u>ee</u>n	l<u>i</u>ke
m<u>i</u>ss	s<u>ea</u>t	w<u>i</u>de
th<u>i</u>nk	pl<u>ea</u>se	m<u>y</u>
g<u>i</u>ve	th<u>e</u>se	t<u>y</u>pe
ph<u>y</u>sical	h<u>e</u>re	t<u>i</u>ny
t<u>y</u>pical	h<u>e</u>ro	s<u>i</u>gn
b<u>ui</u>ld	sh<u>ee</u>t	<u>i</u>sland
pr<u>e</u>tty	pol<u>i</u>ce	l<u>ie</u>
b<u>u</u>sy	c<u>ei</u>ling	h<u>ei</u>ght
<u>E</u>nglish	fi<u>e</u>ld	b<u>uy</u>
b<u>ee</u>n	p<u>eo</u>ple	s<u>i</u>ze
w<u>o</u>men	sk<u>i</u>	r<u>i</u>ght

/e/	/ey/	/ae/
red	place	add
fell	ate	glad
bread	ache	cash
weather	tape	back
many	plain	ran
any	eight	camp
meant	weight	grass
said	neighbor	happy
says	patient	plan
friend	great	had
guess	cafe	angle
end	straight	plaid

/ow/	/o/	/oy/
t<u>ow</u>n	n<u>o</u>	j<u>oy</u>
cr<u>ow</u>d	c<u>o</u>ld	b<u>oy</u>
v<u>ow</u>el	m<u>o</u>re	p<u>oi</u>nt
all<u>ow</u>	c<u>oa</u>t	v<u>oi</u>ce
dr<u>ow</u>n	<u>ow</u>e	destr<u>oy</u>
fl<u>ow</u>er	thr<u>ow</u>	ann<u>oy</u>
s<u>ou</u>nd	fl<u>oor</u>	t<u>oi</u>let
l<u>ou</u>d	th<u>ough</u>	v<u>oy</u>age
<u>ou</u>r	l<u>oa</u>d	av<u>oi</u>d
h<u>ou</u>se	<u>oar</u>	Detr<u>oi</u>t
fl<u>our</u>	gr<u>ow</u>	c<u>oi</u>n
c<u>ou</u>ch	c<u>oa</u>ch	p<u>oi</u>son

/u/	/uw/	/yuw/
p<u>u</u>sh	d<u>o</u>	m<u>u</u>sic
l<u>oo</u>k	wh<u>o</u>	<u>u</u>sual
sh<u>ou</u>ld	ch<u>oo</u>se	<u>U</u>tah
f<u>u</u>ll	f<u>oo</u>l	f<u>ew</u>
f<u>oo</u>t	y<u>ou</u>	c<u>ue</u>
c<u>oo</u>k	fr<u>ui</u>t	men<u>u</u>
w<u>o</u>man	l<u>oo</u>se	h<u>u</u>ge
c<u>ou</u>ld	thr<u>ough</u>	comm<u>u</u>nity
b<u>u</u>ll	gl<u>ue</u>	b<u>eau</u>ty
br<u>oo</u>k	sh<u>oe</u>	m<u>u</u>seum
st<u>oo</u>d	fl<u>ew</u>	v<u>iew</u>
w<u>ou</u>ld	cr<u>ew</u>	p<u>u</u>re

/k/	/ch/	/sh/
keep	child	ship
neck	inch	wash
make	watch	show
college	catch	sure
public	reach	sugar
break	which	special
ache	cheese	Chicago
success	much	ocean
school	cheap	motion
rock	cello	chef
liquor	actual	sheep
stomach	picture	tension

/-s/	/-z/	/-iz/
help<u>s</u>	doe<u>s</u>	watch<u>es</u>
like<u>s</u>	goe<u>s</u>	miss<u>es</u>
laugh<u>s</u>	see<u>s</u>	please<u>s</u>
want<u>s</u>	i<u>s</u>	use<u>s</u>
start<u>s</u>	learn<u>s</u>	push<u>es</u>
stop<u>s</u>	throw<u>s</u>	place<u>s</u>
look<u>s</u>	need<u>s</u>	wish<u>es</u>
keep<u>s</u>	pull<u>s</u>	freeze<u>s</u>
cough<u>s</u>	seem<u>s</u>	catch<u>es</u>
stuff<u>s</u>	sing<u>s</u>	seize<u>s</u>
pick<u>s</u>	hear<u>s</u>	confuse<u>s</u>
wait<u>s</u>	save<u>s</u>	close<u>s</u>

/-t/	**/-d/**	**/-id/**
ask<u>ed</u>	liv<u>ed</u>	need<u>ed</u>
help<u>ed</u>	pleas<u>ed</u>	wait<u>ed</u>
lik<u>ed</u>	listen<u>ed</u>	want<u>ed</u>
push<u>ed</u>	learn<u>ed</u>	count<u>ed</u>
stopp<u>ed</u>	us<u>ed</u>	start<u>ed</u>
cook<u>ed</u>	pull<u>ed</u>	add<u>ed</u>
watch<u>ed</u>	answer<u>ed</u>	land<u>ed</u>
laugh<u>ed</u>	return<u>ed</u>	hat<u>ed</u>
look<u>ed</u>	seem<u>ed</u>	trad<u>ed</u>
plac<u>ed</u>	clos<u>ed</u>	heat<u>ed</u>
pass<u>ed</u>	sav<u>ed</u>	shout<u>ed</u>
cough<u>ed</u>	play<u>ed</u>	vot<u>ed</u>

First*	Second*	Third*
pronoun	pronounce	understand
dictionary	another	explanation
different	agreement	occupation
adjective	direction	absolutely
language	successful	composition
televison	translation	curiosity
document	vocabulary	comprehend
feedback	explosion	democratic
frequently	imagine	disappointed
consonant	inspection	independent
curious	computer	entertain
politics	political	politician

*syllable stressed

Scrambles

Brief Description:

The students re-arrange jumbled sentences, sequences, and stories, for example:

| the | go | they | downtown | in | Do | afternoon | ? |

Each word and punctuation mark is written on a separate card. To make the game easier, the first word can be capitalized and the punctuation mark can be included with the last word of the sentence.

Purpose:

This game is useful for reviewing word and sentence order and the placement of punctuation marks.

Preparation:

The game with sentences is more effective if it concentrates on a single sentence pattern, for example, questions in the present tense. When using the samples of scrambled sentences in this book, cut out the sentence strips from your photocopy and then cut out the individual words, pasting them on separate cards. When developing original material, write out a sentence with each word on a separate card. You can capitalize the first word in the sentence as in the samples. For sequences and stories, write each step or sentence on a separate card.

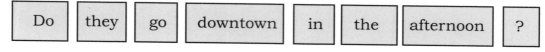

To keep the various sentences from becoming mixed up, it is useful to write a number on each card, either on the face of the card, or on the back, for example:

Five to ten sentences will be sufficient for an interesting game. For the scrambled sentences, each word can be written on a half-card.

Scrambles

Preparation, continued:

Shuffle the cards in each sentence and put a rubber band around each sentence. Finally, make a list of all the sentences for your own reference and for use in step # 5 below.

Procedure:

1. Divide the class into groups of 2 to 3 students.

2. Give each group a sentence and put the extra bundled sentences in a central place.

3. Tell each group to use all the cards to form a sentence.

4. When a group is satisfied with its sentence, they write the number of the sentence and the sentence on a separate sheet of paper. Then the group returns its sentence to the central pile and chooses a new bundle of cards.

5. When the groups have finished, read the correct sentences an have the groups check their answers.

Variations:

1. Have the groups read their answer sheets to each other.

2. The first group to finish can write their answers on the board.

Suggestions:

1. verb tenses*

2. question sentences

3. negative sentences

4. modal auxiliaries

5. passive voice

6. tag questions

7. gerunds and infinitives

8. embedded sentences

9. indirect speech

10. conditional sentences*

11. adverbial clauses*

12. comparatives*

13. superlatives

14. conjunctive adverbs*

15. operations (sequences of actions)*

16. anecdotes and stories*

*** *Photocopyable sample games on these topics are included on the following pages.***

Srambled Sentences: simple present tense

1. I get an email from her every week .

2. He always eats breakfast at 7:30 in the morning .

3. I prefer orange juice , but she likes coffee .

4. He doesn't like the food in the cafeteria .

5. Do you go to the movies every Saturday ?

Srambled Sentences: simple present tense

6. What do you usually do on Sunday afternoons ?

7. What time do you get up in the morning ?

8. Where do they go for their English lessons ?

9. Is this the best way to San Jose ?

10. Doesn't she like her new apartment on Main Street ?

Note: Use a maximum of 10 cards.

Scrambled Sentences: simple past tense

1. Yesterday they flew to Chicago with their friends .

2. We saw them at the beach last Saturday afternoon .

3. Several students were absent from school yesterday afternoon .

4. I bought my computer at that store last weekend .

5. We went to New York to see a play .

Scrambled Sentences: simple past tense

6. I didn't go to class , but Joe did .

7. Did you watch the movie on TV last night ?

8. Did you send an email to your brother yesterday ?

9. She didn't call her family in Venezuela last night .

10. Where were you when you heard the news ?

Note: Use a maximum of 10 cards.

Scrambled Sentences: present perfect tense

1. He hasn't had time to do his homework yet .

2. How long have you lived in this town ?

3. She has lived in this big house since 1995 .

4. Have you ever met the man who lives there ?

5. She has just returned from a vacation in Mexico .

Scrambled Sentences: present perfect tense

6. I have studied English here for almost five years .

7. My friend has never had a driver's license .

8. We have just finished a very difficult lesson .

9. I have never been in this place before .

10. We haven't ever eaten in that famous restaurant .

Note: Use a maximum of 12 cards.

Scrambled Sentences: past perfect tense

1. They had just finished dinner when her friend finally arrived .

2. After he had been there two weeks , he went home .

3. Had you ever studied English before you came here ?

4. They weren't hungry , but I hadn't eaten anything .

5. I had lived there a year before I could speak fluently .

Scrambled Sentences: past perfect tense

6. Before you came here , had you ever had a computer ?

7. I had owned three cars before I bought that one .

8. We had never seen Washington until my uncle took us there .

9. My friends had already left when we came to their house .

10. I had never flown , but I wasn't nervous at all .

Note: Use a maximum of 12 cards.

Scrambled Sentences: conditionals

1. I would not have been angry if you had told the truth.

2. He would not have had that accident if he had been careful.

3. If the doctor calls, please take his number for me.

4. If I had studied harder, I would have passed the test.

5. She could have visited you if she had had more time.

Scrambled Sentences: conditionals

6. If I had invited you, would you have come?

7. If I were president, I would live in the White House.

8. Will you have to travel a lot if you take that job?

9. If it were not so late, I would stay longer.

10. We should leave without him if he doesn't come soon.

Note: Period not on a separate card

Scrambled Sentences: adverbial clauses

1. They had an accident while they were driving to California .

2. What were you doing yesterday when I called ?

3. The fire started while we were studying in the library .

4. We had a flat tire while we were crossing the bridge .

5. I was feeling better when the doctor finally arrived .

Scrambled Sentences: adverbial clauses

6. We got married while she was studying for her Ph D .

7. The wind was blowing hard when I got up this morning .

8. We were watching TV when the dog began to bark .

9. I was taking a shower when the doorbell rang .

10. While Jim was mowing the lawn , we prepared dinner .

Note: Use a maximum of 12 cards, commas and periods on separate cards.

Scrambled Sentences: comparatives

1.	She is taller than I am, but shorter than Carlos.
2.	Her hair is longer than her sister's.
3.	Is the Amazon River wider than the Mississippi?
4.	Is the Chinese language more difficult than English?
5.	The weather this afternoon is worse than it was earlier.

Scrambled Sentences: comparatives

6. Is priority mail faster than first class?

7. I'm feeling much better than I did this morning.

8. I think New York is much more interesting than London.

9. Riding in a car is more dangerous than flying.

10. Is the internet more useful than an encyclopedia?

Note: Use a maximum of 10 cards, punctuation not on separate cards.

Scrambled Sentences: conjunctive adverbs

1. I was given a free ticket to the concert; otherwise, I would not have gone.

2. His mother does not like pets; therefore, he can't have a dog.

3. I used to prefer shopping with cash;

Scrambled Sentences: conjunctive adverbs

however, | now | I | use | a | credit | card.

4. She | had | never | skied | before; | nevertheless, | she | didn't | fall | once.

5. Nobody | knew | the | meaning | of | the | word; | furthermore, | it | wasn't | in | the | dictionary.

Note: Use a maximum of 9 cards, punctuation not on separate cards.

Scrambled Sequence: an operation using a fast food drive-through

Drive to the pick-up window.

Pay for the food.

Take your food.

Roll up your window and leave.

Drive to the menu sign.

Open your window.

Wait for a voice.

Order your food.

Scrambled Sequence: Ahmed's day

Ahmed left his house at 7:30 this morning.

He took his car to the train station and parked it there.

Then he got on the train and rode for one hour to the city.

When he arrived in the city, he got off the train.

Next, he walked two blocks to his office.

He arrived at 8:55.

At 9:00 he sat down at his desk and began to work.

After working for an hour or so, he took a coffee break.

After that, he went back to his desk.

For lunch he went to the Corner Cafe.

After lunch he went back to work.

At last, it was 5:00.

When he left the office, he went to Pedro's Sports Bar.

Finally, he left the bar for the train station.

Unfortunately, he missed the 6:00 train and got home late.

Scrambled Story: *Aesop's "The Lion and the Boar"*

It was a very hot day.
A lion and a boar were very thirsty.
They went to a water hole for a drink.
They saw each other and began to argue.
"I was here first," said the boar.
"I am the king," replied the lion.
They began to fight.
Just then they looked up into the sky.
They saw buzzards coming from every direction.
They were beginning to circle overhead.
"I think it is better to share," said the lion.
"I think so, too," replied the boar.

Scrambled Story: Nasreddin Hodja

Hodja was once a judge.

One day a man came to his house.

The man complained about his neighbor.

Hodja listened carefully.

Then he said, "My good man, you are right."

The man went away happy.

A second man came to see Hodja.

He complained about the first man.

Hodja listened carefully to him, too.

Then he said to the second man, "My good man, you are right."

Hodja's wife had been listening.

After the second man left, she spoke to Hodja.

"Hodja, you told both men they were right.

That's impossible.

They both can't be right."

Hodja listened carefully to his wife.

Then he said to her, "My dear, you are right."

Scrambled Story: A Truckload of Penguins

One day a large truck filled with one hundred penguins broke down on the highway outside a large city. The driver of the truck was trying to decide what to do when a man driving a big, empty bus stopped and offered to help.

The truck driver said, "I have to take these penguins to the zoo right away.

If you will take them in your bus, I'll give you two hundred dollars."

The bus driver agreed to take them.

He put all the penguins into his bus and drove away. Later that afternoon, after he had repaired his truck, the truck driver was driving through the city

when he saw the bus driver with the hundred penguins.

He was walking along the sidewalk followed by the penguins walking two by two in a line.

The truck driver stopped immediately.

He got out of his truck and said to the bus driver, "I told you to take the penguins to the zoo!"

"I did," replied the bus driver, "but I had some money left over, so now I'm taking them to the movies."

Scrambled Story: Clever Hiroshi

One day a clever man named Hiroshi went to a restaurant and ordered Japanese noodles. After he had eaten, he asked for his check, which came to sixteen yen.

He decided that he did not want to pay this amount, so he took out his wallet and counted out the money into the waiter's hand.

"One, two, three, four, five, six, seven, eight...," he said.

He paused and asked the waiter what time it was. "Nine," said the waiter.

"Ten, eleven, twelve, thirteen, fourteen, fifteen, sixteen," continued Hiroshi.

The waiter didn't notice that he had been cheated out of one yen.

Another man who was sitting in the restaurant observed what had happened. He thought this was a good trick and decided to try it.

The next afternoon he returned to the restaurant and ordered Japanese noodles.

When it a came time to pay, he started counting the money into the waiter's hand, just as Hiroshi had done. "One, two, three, four, five, six, seven, eight...," he said.

Then he paused, just as Hiroshi had done, and asked the waiter what time it was.

"Four," the waiter replied.

With that, the man resumed counting, "Five, six, seven, eight, nine, ten, eleven, twelve, thirteen, fourteen, fifteen, sixteen."

Categories

Brief Description:

A student is given a card with several words all belonging to one category, for example, "Things That Are Red." The student makes up clues so that teammates can guess the words on the card.

Purpose:

This game requires the students to use English quickly and descriptively. It can also review vocabulary. It is a good exercise for stretching the students' command of the language as they work under pressure.

Preparation:

Use the cards given, or make up several original cards. Write a category at the top of each card. Then write on the cards four to six words fitting the categories. Easier categories might be "Colors" or " Things in the Classroom." More difficut ones are "Phrasal Verbs with *Put*" or "Things a farmer uses." Easy categories can be made more difficult by putting in one difficult word.

Procedure:

1. Divide the class into two or more teams.

2. Give one card to a member from one of the teams. This person is the clue-giver. Leave the room with the clue-giver to be sure they understand the meanings of the words on the card.

3. The clue-giver announces the category to their own team. The other team(s) watch and listen.

4. The clue-giver then makes up clues while team members try to guess the words on the card. For example, the clue-giver might say, "It is in the sky and gives us heat and light." The team answers with "the sun." Gestures cannot be used.

5. The game continues until all the words have been identified.

6. When the first team is finished, the next team gets a chance to play with a different card.

7. Four or five rounds is usually enough for a good game.

Variations:

1. The clue-giver can be limited to one or two clues, for example, "This vegetable is green and round and you cook it." "A pea!" "No, it is long and thin and about as big as a finger." "A green bean!" "Right." The team can be given a point for each correct answer.

2. The game can be timed. One minute for easy games and up to three minutes for more difficult ones.

3. The teams that are watching can be shown the card to increase their interest as the guessing team tries to get the words.

4. Some of the games can be played as charades. The clue-giver says the category, and then uses gestures only.

Suggestions:

1. Things that are (colors) red, green*, blue.

2. Things that are (sizes) large, small, wide, long, narrow, long and narrow.

3. Things that are typically (nationality) American*, Mexican, Italian, Thai.

4. Things that are found in a (place) classroom*, hotel, park, university*, city, state*, jewelry store*, factory, sea*, kitchen*.

5. Things that are (adjective) funny, easy, round, striped, soft, hot*, expensive.

6. Things that a (profession) teacher, doctor, carpenter*, farmer, etc. needs/uses.

7. Parts of speech — nouns, verbs, adjectives, phrasal verbs*.

8. Things you need to travel*, study, use a computer.

9. Things with a hole*, motor, hair.

10. Things you travel in/on*.

11. Words that begin/end with the letter, a, b, c, etc*.

12. Things to play*, read*, study, watch, listen to*, ride.

13. Things that are part of summer, fall, winter*, spring.

14. Things above*, below, around you.

15. Things used by a man, woman, child*.

16. Things that are eaten, driven, opened*, read, worn.

17. Things to do with your body, feet*, hands.

18. Names of professions*, countries, languages, cities, clothing*, body parts*, food*, fruit, vegetables*, famous people, furniture*, animals*, appliances*, relatives,* stores*, parts of a car*, sports*.

19. Computer commands*, hardware, software.

Photocopyable games on these topics are included on the following

Things That Are Green

grass

lettuce

peppers

trees

peas

dollars

Things above You

sky

ceiling

moon

roof

stars

sun

Things That Are Found in a Classroom

chalk

students

blackboard

desks

teacher

books

Animals

deer

goat

bear

skunk

squirrel

tiger

Things That You Travel in

car

train

ship

airplane

taxi

bus

Vegetables

squash

corn

tomatos

beans

spinach

cucumbers

Clothing

shirt

pants

socks

underwear

shoes

hat

Food

spaghetti

steak

salad

potato

rice

pizza

Parts of the Body

arm

leg

finger

shoulder

knee

chest

Stores

hardware

grocery

drug

music

clothing

shoe

**Things You Do
with Your Feet**

walk

kick

jump

dance

run

ski

Sports

baseball

basketball

volleyball

golf

soccer

softball

Furniture	**Things That You Listen to**
sofa	radio
table	teacher
bed	CD
dresser	friend
coffee table	advice
armchair	jokes

Relatives	**Winter Things**
aunt	snow
cousin	skiing
nephew	ice
grandmother	boots
niece	snowboards
brother-in-law	scarf

Things You Find in a Kitchen	**Things That Are Used by a Child**
sink	toy
toaster	tricycle
napkins	mittens
silverware	kite
microwave	shorts
blender	blocks

Things You Play

soccer

guitar

games

piano

cards

volleyball

Things You Need for Traveling

suitcase

photo ID

money

ticket

credit card

map

Words That Begin with "f"

friend

flower

fly

France

fat

finger

Things That Are Hot

oven

summer

desert

coffee

steam

light bulb

Things That Are Typically American

hamburgers

baseball

hot dogs

Coca Cola

apple pie

doughnuts

Things That You Find at a University

dormitory

cafeteria

gym

stadium

student union

health center

Things That a
Carpenter Needs or Uses
hammer

nails

saw

toolbox

tape measure

drill

Professions
scientist

lawyer

accountant

surgeon

dentist

psychiatrist

Appliances
iron

hair dryer

toaster oven

can opener

freezer

coffee maker

Phrasal Verbs
call up

hang up

look like

run into

do over

get along with

Things That Are
Opened
letter

can

gift

closet

checking account

refrigerator

Things in
a Jewelry Store
necklace

watch

ring

bracelet

diamond

pearls

Things You Find in Florida

- oranges
- beaches
- alligators
- space shuttles
- palm trees
- theme parks

Things Found in the Sea

- reefs
- whales
- dolphins
- seaweed
- shrimp
- squid

Things with holes

- bagel
- Swiss cheese
- golf course
- nose
- bath tub
- bottle

Things to Read

- novel
- poem
- short story
- email
- journal
- paperback

Parts of a Car

- battery
- radiator
- brake
- muffler
- gas tank
- air bag

Computer Commands

- save
- delete
- open
- find
- cut and paste
- insert table

Scenarios

Brief Description:

This is a role-playing exercise in which each participant receives a card describing a character whose identity they assume. At the conclusion of the exerecise the class identifies and describes the various people they have met. The lives of the characters can be entwined or a plot can unfold to make the exercise more interesting.

Purpose:

The exercise requires the students to practice social conversation. It also requires them to listen carefully and at the end of the exercise, remember and re-state what they have heard.

Preparation:

It is a good idea to experiment with this technique by trying some of the sample materials given in this book. When developing your own Scenarios, write brief descriptions on the cards — one to a card. The game is best played by at least six and not more than sixteen characters. In a game designed for a lower level class, only a minimum of information — such as name, age, profession — should be given.

Senarios

Procedure:

1. Give the directions to the students. First, set the context of the scenario — reunion, party, meeting, bus station, etc.

2. Give each student a card and ask them to study it.

3. In a quiet corner or outside the room, help the students with any questions they might have.

4. Let the students mingle and talk to each other for 15 to 30 minutes.

5. When it seems that everybody has met everybody else, conclude the game.

6. Single out each character, one by one, and have the other students tell what they can remember about the character.

Variations:

1. At the end of the game, have the students write out the cast of characters, and then read their papers to each other and compare results.

2. A position on a contemporary issue can be added to the information on each card. In this way, finding out each character's opinion on the issue becomes part of the game's objective.

3. In a multilingual class, the students can work in pairs. One student speaks their native language and their partner acts as an interpreter.

Suggestions:

1. Family tree — the students construct a family tree.*

2. Family gatherings — relationships are discovered.*

3. Neighborhood party — local gossip, entanglements, social concerns are learned.

4. School party — weekend plans, life goals are discovered.

5. Bus/airplane trip — passengers discover how their lives are entwined.*

6. Murder mystery — a group of people discover a murder and decide "whodunnit."*

7. Reunion — old classmates rediscover and catch up with each other.

8. Meeting — an important decison is discussed and made.

Photocopyable games on these topics are included on the following pages.

Family Tree

Gavin Morgan 1970	Sven Bergstrom 1908
Heather Antonelli-Morgan 1970	Olga Bergstrom 1910
Arthur Morgan 1940	Alberto Antonelli 1903
Isabelle B. Morgan 1942	Marie Doucette 1905
Luigi Antonelli 1946	Sean O' Brien 1917
Mary O'Brien Antonelli 1947	Mary McDonald 1918
Benjamin Morgan 1905	Alfred Morgan 1865
Mariette Van Slyke 1904	Claude Doucette 1880

Note: The dates given are birthdates.
With fewer than 16 students, use the cards
from the top left of the page down.

Family Gathering

Harold Pinton – 45 years old Married, 3 children	Nora Pinton – 21 years old You have a twin sister
Virginia Pinton – 42 years old Married to Harold Pinton	Steve Pinton – 18 years old Your mother is Virginia Pinton. You have two sisters
Nancy Pinton – 21 years old Father is Harold Pinton	Alex Owens – 72 years old Virginia Pinton is your niece
Jeff Pinton – 15 years old Your mother is Barbara Pinton	Anne Owens – 42 years old Harold is your brother-in-law
Barbara Pinton – 38 years old Wife of Mark Pinton	Martha Pinton – 74 years old Your grandson is Jeff
George Owens – 70 years old You have one daughter who is married to Harold Pinton	Andy Pinton – 17 years old You are Harold Pinton's neph- ew
Mark Pinton – 40 years old Son of John Pinton	Phyllis Pinton – 22 years old Nora is your cousin
John Pinton – 75 years old You have two sons — Harold and Mark	Greg Pinton – 19 years old You have two brothers

Note: You do not need 16 people to play this game.
The first eight characters in the left column are basic.
Add others in sequence as you need them.

Murder Mystery

Note: At first everyone should introduce themselves to each other, but they should reveal the information in italics to the detectives only.

Martin Danfield. You are a very wealthy man. You are also a womanizer. You are having a birthday party for your daughter, Leslie. You are very angry with your son, and you refuse to speak to him. *After you finish your first drink, you die. Someone in the room has poisoned you.*

Sally Danfield. You married Martin Danfield two years ago. You are much younger than Martin. You married him for his money, and you will inherit it when he dies. *You suspect that he is seeing another woman.*

Marsha Danfield. You have two children from your marriage with Martin Danfield. After you were married for 37 years, he asked you for a divorce so that he could marry a younger woman. *You have never forgiven him for that.*

Benjamin Danfield. You are the son of Martin and Marsha Danfield. You are vice-president of your father's business. You often go to Las Vegas because you love to gamble. *Your father is going to fire you because he has discovered that you have stolen a lot of money from the business to pay your gambling debts.*

Carla Fleming. You are married to Chester Fleming. You are Martin Danfield's personal secretary, and you often accompany him on business trips. *You have had a long, secret affair with Martin, but on the last trip he told you it was over and asked you to resign.*

Chester Fleming. You are Martin Danfield's old friend. Your wife is his personal secretary. *You have discovered that Martin has carried on an affair with your wife for many years. You have poisoned his drink.*

Leslie Ellworth. Your father is Martin Danfield. You are married to Dunton Ellsworth, who worked for your father until a year ago when your father fired him without warning. Dunton has become an alcoholic. *You hate your father for what he has done to your husband.*

Detective Dan Brown. You arrive at the party after Martin Danfield dies. You ask each of the guests to identify themselves. Then you interview them one at a time. Based on your interviews you will try to discover the murderer.

Detective George Green. You assist your partner Dan Brown in the investigation.

Airplane Trip

Pedro Fernandez. You are a Mexican businessman who imports televisions from Europe. You are returning to Mexico after a business trip to New York. You wanted to begin importing American televisions, but you weren't successful.

Maria Fernandez. You are the wife of Pedro Fernandez. Ten years ago, a young American named Yvonne stayed in your house in Guadalajara, Mexico. You haven't seen her since then.

Yvonne Addley. You are married to Donald Addley. Ten years ago, when you were single, you spent a summer in Mexico. You stayed with the family of Pedro Fernenadez. You plan to visit your Mexican family and introduce them to your husband.

Donald Addley. You and your wife are going to Mexico for a vacation. You have just finished your Ph D, and you are hoping to get a job in the English department at the University of Northfield.

Peggy Wallace. You plan to study medicine in Mexico. You are going to have an interview at the University of Guadalajara. After that you are going to have a vacation in Cancun.

Dr. Carlos Garcia. You are returning to Mexico after a trip to New York. You are Director of Admissions at the University of Guadalajara. You went to high school with Pedro Fernandez.

Toshihiro Sato. You export televisions from Japan. You are going to Mexico to find an importer. You studied English and Spanish ten years ago at the Tokyo Language Center. After a week in Guadalajara, you will take a vacation in Cancun, where you have rented a villa.

Alice King. Ten years ago you lived in Japan and taught English and Spanish at the Tokyo Language Center. You recognize Toshihiro as one of your former students. Several years ago you studied Spanish at the University of Guadalajara.

David King. You and your wife, Alice, are going to Mexico for a vacation. You are planning to end your vacation in Cancun. You are Chair of the English Department at the University of Northfield.

Ted Ward. You are one of the stewards on the flight to Mexico. Years ago, you dated Alice King when the two of you studied Spanish in Guadalajara. Maria Fernandez was your teacher. Peggy Wallace is your girl friend.

Love Boat Cruise

Melinda, 28.

Single. Travel agent. Loves beaches, shopping, flying.

Traveling with a friend.

Nancy, 25.

Single. Works for Ad agency. Loves reading, art galleries, the theater. Traveling with a friend.

Don, 28.

Single. Owns dot.com. Loves islands, the internet, has a pilot's licence. Traveling with business partner.

Tim, 29.

Single. Owns dot.com. Loves painting, does book reviews, is an amateur actor. Traveling with business partner.

Grace, 55.

Widow. Wealthy. Has apartment in Manhattan, many investments, loves fine restaurants.

Traveling with daughter.

George, 58.

Widower. Loves city life, gourmet dining, investing in the stock market. Traveling with son.

Susannah, 31.

Single. Loves the cinema, playing scrabble, long walks in the morning. Traveling with mother.

Arthur, 30.

Single. Loves chess, going to the gym, and has extensive video collection. Traveling with father.

Francine, 40.

Divorced. Loves dancing, cruises, horses. Traveling with sister.

Jenny, 38.

Single. Loves hiking, running, and dogs. Traveling with sister.

Pat, 45.

Divorced. Loves night life, the race track, and yachting. Traveling with brother.

Mike, 40.

Single. Loves tennis, backpacking, and cats. Traveling with brother.

Pyramids

Brief Description:

On each card there is a question and its answer on the same side of the card. A player draws a card and asks an opponent the question. The opponent tries to answer, and the first player looks at the answer on the card and decides if the opponent's answer is right or wrong. The quiz can be carried out in a variety of formats.

Purpose:

This is a review of subject matter that is either general knowledge or part of the learner's course work. The sample cards which follow were chosen to illustrate the great variety of language and content information students can work with in this game, anything from history or civics to math or science. And while learning the content, the players build confidence and skills.

Preparation:

Prepare a set of 24 cards with a question and its answer on the same side of each card. Try to order the cards from easy to difficult.

Procedure:

1. Place a stack of cards in front of the two opponents (two individuals or two teams), and give each of them a blank pyramid.

2. Player A takes the top card and reads the question to Player B. If Player B answers correctly, Player B puts an X or writes the answer in a box in the base of their pyramid. Then Player B asks Player A the next question in the stack.

3. Play continues as each opponent builds a pyramid from the base to the top. The first player to complete a pyramid wins.

4. If neither player builds a pyramid and all the cards have been used, the player with the most correct answers wins.

5. If one player builds a pyramid and there are still some unused cards, the losing opponent can be given the opportunity to catch up by answering the remaining cards.

_____'s Pyramid

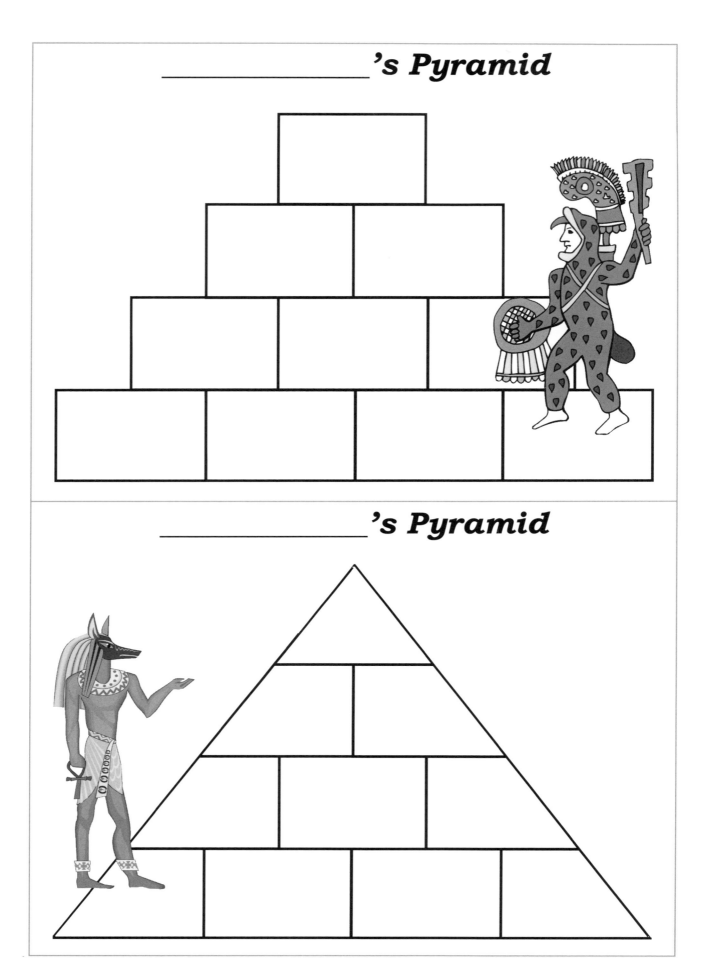

_____'s Pyramid

Variations:

1. The game can be played by two teams competing against each other.

2. The game can be played with a non-playing quizmaster posing the question to both teams. Any player can say "Buzz" for a chance to answer. The first player to buzz tries to answer the question. If the buzzer gives a wrong answer, a player from the opposing team gets a chance to answer. If no one buzzes, play continues to the next card. When all the cards have been used, the team with the most correct answers wins.

3. The teacher can ask the entire class the questions, and the students write their answers. When all the cards have been used, the correct answers are given and a winner is determined.

4. The game can be played with other formats, for example: a simple quiz game, tic-tac-toe, or hangman.

Suggestions:

1. Country facts*

2. World facts*

3. History quiz*

4. Vocabulary relating to a specific lexical area (money*, clothing, vehicles, business, agriculture)

5. Verb forms — "What is the past tense of 'begin'?"

6. Idioms — "Tried and true."*

7. Proverbs — "The grass is always greener . . . ."*

8. Measurements — "How many pints in a quart?"*

9. Famous people, books, songs, films*

*__Photocopyable sample games on these topics are included
on the following pages.__

Measurements

1. How many inches are there in one foot? — *Twelve*	7. How many cups are there in one pint? — *Two*
2. How many feet are there in one yard? — *Three*	8. How many days in a leap year? — *366*
3. How many ounces are there in one pound? — *Sixteen*	9. How many months have 31 days? — *Seven*
4. How many pounds are there in one ton? — *2000*	10. Which is longer, one yard or one meter? — *One meter*
5. How many quarts are there in one gallon? — *Four*	11. How many inches in a square foot? — *144*
6. How many pints are there in one Quart? — *Two*	12. Which is longer, one mile or one kilometer? — *One mile*

Measurements

13. One kilogram is about: 1.2, 2.2, 3.2, pounds. — *2.2*	19. Ten years is one: century, decade, score. — *Decade*
14. 100 kilometers per hour is about: 50, 60, 70 miles per hour. — *60*	20. How many years in a milennium? — *1000*
15. Water freezes at: 0, 32, 65 degrees fahrenheit. — *32°*	21. What is the numerical value of pi? — *Approximately 3.14*
16. 10 degrees Celsius is about: 20, 50, 70 degrees fahrenheit. — *50°*	22. What is the meaning of Mach 1? — *The speed of sound*
17. How many feet in one mile? — *5,280*	23. What is the speed of light? — *Approximately 186,000 miles per second/ 300,000 km per second.*
18. What is the abbreviation for pound? — *lb.*	24. How long is a marathon? — *Approximately 26 miles/ 41.3 kilometers.*

Ameriquiz: set A

1. How many states in the United States of America? — *50*	7. In which state is Disneyworld? — *Florida*
2. What is the largest state? — *Alaska*	8. In which state is Chicago? — *Illinois*
3. Which state has the smallest population? — *Wyoming*	9. In which state is Great Salt Lake? — *Utah*
4. Which state is farthest east? — *Maine*	10. Where is Death Valley? — *California*
5. In which state is Boston? — *Massachusetts*	11. Where is Yellowstone National Park? — *Wyoming*
6. In which city is Wall Street? — *New York City*	12. Name the New England States. — *New Hampshire, Maine, Vermont, Massachusetts, Connecticut, Rhode Island*

Ameriquiz: Set A

13. Which state is not on the Atlantic Ocean: New Jersey, North Carolina, or Kentucky?   — *Kentucky*

19. How many lakes are there in the Great Lakes?
— *five*

14. What is the longest river in The United States?
— *The Mississippi*

20. What river separates the US and Canada?
— *The St. Lawrence*

15. Are the Appalachian Mountains in the eastern or western part of the US? — *eastern*

21. Which state borders on Mexico? California Utah, Nevada, or Colorado?
— *California*

16. Is Chesapeake Bay on the Atlantic or Pacific Ocean?
— *Atlantic*

22. How many states have a shoreline on the Pacific Ocean? — *four*
(CA, OR, WA, AK)

17. Which state is an island: Hawaii, Michigan, or Rhode Island?
— *Hawaii*

23. Which mountain is a volcano: Mount St.Helens, Mount Washington, or Mount Rushmore? — *Mt. St. Helens*

18. Which state is not on the Gulf of Mexico: South Carolina, Louisiana, or Alabama? — *S. Carolina*

24. What is the highest mountain in Alaska?
— *Denali*

Ameriquiz: set B

1. Which states do not border on any other state? — *Alaska and Hawaii*	7. Where is the Grand Canyon? — *Arizona*
2. What is the smallest state? — *Rhode Island*	8. In which state is Houston? — *Texas*
3. Which state has the largest population? — *California*	9. What lake is between Wisconsin and Michigan? — *Lake Michigan*
4. Which state is farthest west? — *Hawaii*	10. In which state is Cape Canaveral? — *Florida*
5. In which state is Seattle? — *Washington*	11. Where is the Everglades National Park? — *Florida*
6. In which city is the Golden Gate Bridge? — *San Francisco*	12. Which New England state does not have an ocean shoreline? — *Vermont*

Ameriquiz: Set B

13. Which state does not have a border with Canada: Minnesota, Montana, or Oregon? — *Oregon*	**19.** Niagara Falls is between Ontario and . . . ? — *New York*
14. Where is the Yukon River? — *Alaska*	**20.** What city is at the mouth of the Mississippi River? — *New Orleans*
15. Where are the Sierra Nevada Mountains? — *California*	**21.** Which state has a border with Quebec: Maine, North Dakota, or Minnesota? — *Maine*
16. The Mississippi delta is in which state? — *Louisiana*	**22.** How many states have a shoreline on the Gulf of Mexico? — *five* (TX, LA, MS, AL, FL)
17. Which state borders on Russia? — *Alaska*	**23.** Which mountain is in the Rocky Mountains: Rainier, Hood, or Pike's Peak? — *Pike's Peak*
18. Which state has a shoreline on Lake Ontario? — *New York*	**24.** What is the highest mountain in Hawaii? — *Mauna Loa*

Worldquiz

1. What is the principal language of Brazil? — *Portuguese*	7. The country with the largest population in Africa is . . . — *Nigeria*
2. The world's smallest continent and sixth largest country is . . . — *Australia*	8. The invasion of Normandy on June 6, 1944 is also called . . . — *D-Day*
3. The holy city of Mecca is where? — *Saudi Arabia*	9. What is the largest island in the Mediterranean? — *Sicily*
4. Norway, Sweden, and Denmark are often called . . . — *Scandinavia*	10. The Russian Revolution took place in what year? — *1917*
5. What is the dominant religion in Indonesia? — *Islam*	11. India became independent in . . . — *1947*
6. The rising sun is the symbol of what country? — *Japan*	12. Which language isn't official in Switzerland: French, Hungarian, German, or Italian? — *Hungarian*

Worldquiz

13. Which language isn't part of the Indo-European family: Russian, Finnish, Spanish, Hindi, or Farsi? — *Finnish*

19. The largest island in the world, Greenland, is owned by . . .
— *Denmark*

14. During which years was World War I fought ?
— *1914-1918*

20. Where was the Boer War fought?
— *South Africa*

15. What city was the capital of the Ottoman Empire?
— *Istanbul*

21. The Mayan people of Mexico also lived in Honduras, Guatemala, and what other country?   — *Belize*

16. What two countries occupy the island of Hispaniola? — *Haiti and the Dominican Republic*

22. Where was the battle of Marathon fought?
— *Greece*

17. The man known as "The Liberator" of northern South America was...
— *Simon Bolivar*

23. What is the only man-made structure that can be seen from outer space?
— *The Great Wall of China*

18. Where do the majority of the Basque people live?
— *Spain*

24. Where is Mount Everest?
— *Between Nepal and Tibet*

Dynamic Duos

1. ladies and . . . *gentlemen*	7. law and . . . *order*
2. lost and . . . *found*	8. bride and . . . *groom*
3. bacon and . . . *eggs*	9. track and . . . *field*
4. bread and . . . *butter*	10. fun and . . . *games*
5. cut and . . . *paste*	11. back and . . . *forth*
6. hit and . . *run*	12. room and . . . *board*

Dynamic Duos

13. safe and . . . *sound*	19. Romeo and . . . *Juliet*
14. bed and . . . *breakfast*	20. Samson and . . . *Delilah*
15. gin and . . . *tonic*	21. Lewis and . . . *Clark*
16. stop and . . . *go*	22. Hansel and . . . *Gretel*
17. good and . . . *evil*	23. Punch and . . . *Judy*
18. Batman and . . . *Robin*	24. Rodgers and . . . *Hammerstein*

Note: complete the phrase.

Blankety-Blank Idioms

1. I will love you forever and _____

— *ever*

2. It's better late than _____

— *never*

3. I'm going to rest and take a short _____ nap.

— *cat*

4. She can grow anything. She has a _____ thumb.

— *green*

5. It's better to be _____ than sorry.

— *safe*

6. It only happens once in a _____ moon.

— *blue*

7. I'm tired. I'm going to _____ the hay.

— *hit*

8. Get up! It's time to _____ and shine.

— *rise*

9. It was very expensive. It cost an arm and a _____

— *leg*

10. He failed. All his dreams went up in _____

— *smoke*

11. When she left him, he was broken-_____

— *hearted*

12. An optimist sees the world through _____-colored glasses.

— *rose*

Blankety-Blank Idioms

13. He went above and _____ the call of duty.
    — *beyond*

14. When I heard the news it hit me like a _____ of bricks.
    — *ton*

15. It's great to see you. You're a sight for _____ eyes.
    — *sore*

16. Like father, like son: a chip off the _____ block.
    — *old*

17. She wouldn't stop. She talked a _____ streak.
    — *blue*

18. I didn't mean it. It was an honest to _____ mistake.
    — *goodness*

19. I couldn't wake him. He was out like a _____.
    — *light*

20. He made far and _____ the best offer.
    — *away*

21. You have no proof. You're without a _____ to stand on.
    — *leg*

22. When her friend got the prize, she was _____ with envy.
    — *green*

23. I had nothing to drink. I was as sober as a _____.
    — *judge*

24. Come out and fight, you _____-bellied coward.
    — *yellow*

Note: The students can say "blankety-blank," "blank," "something," or "what" in place of the blanks.

Old Wisdom

1. All that glitters . . . — *is not gold.*	7. Let sleeping dogs. . . — *lie.*
2. No news is . . . — *good news.*	8. Don't judge a book... — *by its cover.*
3. Haste makes . . . — *waste.*	9. If the shoe fits, . . . — *wear it.*
4. Look before you . . . — *leap.*	10. Actions speak louder than . . . — *words.*
5. Two heads are better than . . . — *one.*	11. Where there's smoke . . . — *there's fire.*
6. Half a loaf is better than . . . — *none.*	12. People in glass houses, . . . — *shouldn't throw stones.*

Old Wisdom

13. When in Rome, . . . 　— *do as the* 　　*Romans do.*	19. Don't bite the hand . . . 　— *that feeds you.*
14. When the cat's away . . . 　— *the mice* 　　*will play.*	20. Make hay while. . . 　— *the sun shines.*
15. A stitch in time . . . 　— *saves nine.*	21. You can lead a horse to water, but . . . 　— *you can't* 　　*make him drink.*
16. Many hands . . . 　— *make light work.*	22. Rome was not built . . . 　— *in a day.*
17. An apple a day keeps. . . 　— *the doctor away.*	23. Don't count your chickens . . 　— *before they hatch.*
18. A bird in the hand is worth . . 　— *two in the bush.*	24. The early bird catches . . . 　— *the worm.*

U. S. History

1. What group of people came to America on the Mayflower? — *the Pilgrims*	7. Who was the principal writer of the Declaration of Independence? — *Thomas Jefferson*
2. Which holiday is on July 4th? — *Independence Day*	8. The Bill of Rights is part of what document? — *The U.S. Constitution*
3. In what year did the U.S. declare its independence? — *1776*	9. What is the name of the national anthem? — *The Star Spangled Banner*
4. The 13 original states had been colonies of what country? — *England*	10. In what state was the Battle of Lexington and Concord fought? — *Massachusetts*
5. How many stripes are there in the U.S. flag? — *13*	11. Texas was once part of which country? — *Mexico*
6. Which state was not one of the original 13 states: New Hampshire, Georgia, Kentucky, North Carolina? — *Kentucky*	12. Who were Lewis and Clark? — *Explorers of the American West/ the Louisiana Purchase*

U. S. History

13. Who was president during the Civil War? — *Abraham Lincoln*	19. Many immigrants to America landed first on which island? — *Ellis Island*
14. What Civil War general became a U.S. President? — *Ulysses Grant*	20. When did women receive the right to vote? — *1920*
15. Who was Robert E. Lee? — *Commander of the confederate army*	21. Who was president during most of the Second World War? – *Franklin D. Roosevelt*
16. Who signed The Emancipation Proclamation? — *Abraham Lincoln*	22. Which president ordered the atomic bombing of Hiroshima and Nagasaki? — *Harry Truman*
17. Who invented the light bulb? — *Thomas Edison*	23. Which World War II American general became president? — *Dwight Eisenhower*
18. Who built and flew the first airplane? — *The Wright Brothers*	24. Who was the first man to step on the moon? — *Neil Armstrong*

Oscars

1. 2004: Million _____ Baby — *Dollar*	7. 1990: Dances with ___ _____ — *Wolves*
2. 2003: The _____ of the Rings — *Lord*	8. 1988: Rain _____ — *Man*
3. 2001: A _____ Mind — *Beautiful*	9. 1987: The Last _____. — *Emperor*
4. 1998: Shakespeare in _____ — *Love*	10. 1985: Out of _____ — *Africa*
5. 1996: The English _____ — *Patient*	11. 1981: Chariots of _____ — *Fire*
6. 1993: Schindler's _____ — *List*	12. 1978: The Deer _____ — *Hunter*

Oscars

13. 1975:
One Flew Over the
Cuckoo's _____.
    — *Nest*
	19. 1962:
	Lawrence of _____
	    — *Arabia*

14. 1974:
The French _____
    — *Connection*
	20. 1961:
	West Side _____
	    — *Story*

15. 1967: In the Heat
of the _____
    — *Night*
	21. 1956: Around the
	World in Eighty _____
	    — *Days*

16. 1966:
Man for All _____
    — *Seasons*
	22. 1953:
	From Here to _____
	    — *Eternity*

17. 1965:
The Sound of _____
    — *Music*
	23. 1951:
	An American in _____
	    — *Paris*

18. 1964:
My Fair _____
    — *Lady*
	24. 1939: Gone with
	the _____
	    — *Wind*

What is Money?

1. Pieces of money made from metal, usually round, are called _____ — *coins*	7. A _____ person is very rich. — *wealthy*
2. To give money to someone on a temporary basis is called a _____ — *loan*	8. A person who earns $8.00 an hour is a _____earner. — *wage*
3. The charge for loaning money is called _____ — *interest*	9. An _____ hires people to work for them. — *employer*
4. The person who receives a loan is called a _____ — *borrower*	10. The money a person earns is called their annual _____. — *income*
5. To play with money at a casino is called_____ — *gambling*	11. To earn money from doing business is to make a _____. — *profit*
6. Illegally printed money is _____ money. — *counterfeit*	12. To lose money from doing business is to have a _____ — *loss*

What is Money?

13. Selling things to individual customers is _____ business. — *retail*	19. A person who owns stock in a company is a _____holder. — *share*
14. Selling things to people who sell things is a _____ business. — *wholesale*	20. The condition of rising prices is called _____. — *inflation*
15. A person who buys goods and services is a _____ — *consumer*	21. An _____ is something of value that a person or company owns. — *asset*
16. To have no money is to be _____. — *broke*	22. A _____ is something that a person or company owes. — *liability*
17. To make an initial deposit on a purchase is to make a _____ _____. — *down payment*	23. After retirement, a person earns money from a _____. — *pension*
18. To sell something without taking cash is to give _____ — *credit*	24. "Nothing is certain but death and _____." — *taxes*

The students can use "what" in the place of the blanks.

Abbreviations and Acronyms

1. **FBI** *-- Federal Bureau of Investigation*	7. **M.D.** *-- Doctor of Medicine*
2. **NASA** *-- National Air and Space Administration*	8. **Ph. D.** *-- Doctor of Philosophy*
3. **PC** *-- Personal Computer*	9. **B.A.** *-- Bachelor of Arts*
4. **UAE** *— United Arab Emirates*	10. **IRS** *-- Internal Revenue Service*
5. **EU** *-- European Union*	11. **IRA** *-- Individual Retirement Account*
6. **D.C.** *-- District of Columbia*	12. **POW** *-- Prisoner of War*

Abbreviations and Acronyms

13. **CEO** *— Chief Executive Officer*	19. **CIA** *-- Central Intelligence Agency*
14. **C. O. D.** *-- cash on delivery*	20. **FYI** *— for your information*
15. **CPA** *-- Certified Public Accountant*	21. **NATO** *-- North Atlantic Treaty Organization*
16. **DWI** *-- driving while intoxicated*	22. **OPEC** *-- Organization of Petroleum Exporting Countries*
17. **DOA** *-- dead on arrival*	23. **mph** *-- miles per hour*
18. **EPA** *-- Environmental Protection Agency*	24. **PIN** *-- personal identification number*

Students ask: "What is (the) _____?" or "What does _____ stand for?"

Resources

More Index Card Games for English. 9 more games using index cards appropriate for students at different proficiency levels. These games stress speaking and listening skills. As in **Index Card Games for ESL,** though in a smaller format, all the sample material is photocopyable.

Match It! Another photocopyable collection of index card games. The game "Match It!" is similar to "Concentration." The materials range in difficulty from basic/easy to advanced/difficult.

Pronunciation Card Games. A photocopyable collection of index card games working on minimal pairs, syllabification, stress and intonation.

The Great Big Bingo Book. A photocopyable collection of bingo games, providing practice with grammar, vocabulary, writing, pronunciation, and cultural information.

Shenanigames. 49 games practicing specific grammar points of graded difficulty. They are appropriate for students from middle school to adult.

The ESL Miscellany. A single-volume teacher resource book with dozens of lists of grammatical information, vocabulary topics, cultural information, miscellaneous material (punctuation rules, spelling rules, abbreviations, maps, gestures, etc.). A great resource for developing games and other lesson materials.

Lexicarry. Hundreds of uncaptioned pictures which get students talking about language, learning vocabulary, and discussing what language is appropriate in the pictured situations. Includes functions, sequences, operations, topics, and proverbs. Ideal for pair and small group work. A word list in the back allows for self-study. Wordlists in other languages and a teacher's guide are free at www.Lexicarry.com. Over 4500 words.

English Interplay: Surviving. A first text for beginning adolescents and adults. Students work in pairs, triads, and small groups, learning basic grammar, spelling, pronunciation, numbers, and a 700-word vocabulary.

Rhymes and Rhythms. 32 original poems/chants for practicing basic grammar and pronunciation and learning vocabulary. The rhymes progress from short and easy to longer, more challenging. This is a photocopyable text with an optional CD recording of all the rhymes read once deliberately and then read again at natural speed.

Pro Lingua Associates • 800-366-4775 • www.ProLinguaAssociates.com